BIZA DEATHS

FAMOUS INDIVIDUALS AND OTHERS WHO DIED IN HORRIFIC CIRCUMSTANCES

As well as several previously unpublished entries this book contains relevant extracts from our substantial publication "Untimely and Tragic Deaths of the Renowned, the Celebrated, and the Iconic: Featuring Ordinary Individuals Who Died in Bizarre Circumstances".

The contents of this publication may not be produced in whole or part, in any form or by any means, in printed or digital form without written permission from the authors, except for short extracts or quotes which may be used for the purpose of comments or reviews.

Copyright © 2021 BH & VHM McKechnie all rights reserved

Contents

Introduction

List of individuals (alphabetical order)

Entries

Bibliography

Introduction

First published in 2021, this book provides details of individuals from the world of **film, literature, music, sport, theatre, and television**, as well as many **ordinary people**, all of whom died in bizarre, extraordinary, peculiar, strange, or unusual circumstances.

It does not matter if they were famous or just celebrated and loved by a few individuals, all the people in this book left behind family, friends and in some instances devotees who idolised them. Our heartfelt thoughts and sympathies go out to all those affected by each persons death.

There are many conspiracy theories, rumours, cover-ups, allegations, sensationalism, and myths about the cause of some individual's deaths. Only the facts known at the time of writing are included in this book.

List of individuals (alphabetical order)

124 entries

Ace, Johnny (Singer)
Aeschylus (Playwright)
Allman, Duanne (Guitarist)
Allport, Christopher (Actor)
Amundsen, Roald (Explorer)
Anderson, Sherwood (Author)
Andrews, Thomas (Shipbuilder)
Arkeen, West (Musician)

Ballard, Florence (Singer)
Ballard, Sam (Rugby Player)
Belk, Lottie Michelle (Not known)
Bernecker, John (Stuntman)
Betts, James (Student)
Biaksangzula, Peter (Footballer)
Biggs, Gregory Glenn (Not known)
Bonham, John Henry (Drummer)

Bowman, Mildred (Not known)

Brahe, Tycho (Astronomer)

Brenno, Jeremy T (Not known)

Brohm, Francis Daniel (Not known)

Brown, Basil (Health Food Enthusiast)

Budlong, Jack (Movie extra)

Buckley, Jeff (Singer)

Burduchenko, Inna (Actress)

Burger, Rebecca (Fitness blogger)

Burrus, Joseph (Escape Artist)

Burton, Cliff (Musician)

Castle, Vernon (Ballroom dancer)

Chaibancha, Mitr (Stuntman)

Chaney, Lon (Actor)

Charondas (Lawgiver)

Cooke, Sam (Singer)

Cooper, Tommy (Comedian)

Croce, Jim (Singer)

Cummings, John (Sailor)

Daniel, Jack (Distiller)
Di Paolo, Renato (Actor)
Didenko, Valenti (Not known)
Disi, Salvatore (Pilot)
Driscoll, Bobby (Actor)
Draco of Athens (Lawgiver)
Duncan, Isadora (Dancer)

Earhart, Amelia (Pilot)
Edwards, Mike (Cellist)
Edwards, Richey (Guitarist)
Entwistle, Peg (Actress)

Findlay, Michael (Producer)

Garcia, Joana Sainz (Dancer)
Gingrich, Greg Austin (Not known)
Glynn, Molly (Actress)
Godel, Kurt Friedrich (Mathematician)
Grundman, David (Not known)

Harron, Robert (Actor)
Harvey, Leslie Cameron (Guitarist)
Hayes, Frank (Horse trainer)
Hernandez, Humberto (Not known)
Herzberg, Elaine (Not known)
Heselden, Jimi (Entrepreneur)
Hexum, Jon-Erik (Actor)
Hiromi, Katsuki (Actress)
Houdini, Harry (Escapologist)
Hoy, Gary (Lawyer)

Irwin, Steve (TV personality)

Johnson, Robert (Singer)
Jordan, John (Cameraman)

Kath, Terry (Musician)
Keilberth, Joseph (Orchestral Conductor)
Kivlenieks, Mattis Edmunds (Ice Hockey Goaltender)

Lam, Elisa (Student)
Larsson, Stig (Writer)
Lazear, Jesse William (Physician)
Leach, Bobby (Daredevil)
Lee, Brandon (Actor)
Lee Mr (Unknown)
Lully, Jean-Baptiste (Composer)

MacColl, Kirsty (Singer)
Mansfield, Martha (Actress)
Mantell, Thomas Francis (Pilot)
Mathilda of Austria (Unknown)
McGuire, Ivan Lester (Parachutist)
McHugh, Grace (Actress)
Meinsenheimer, Brenda Lee (Actress)
Metcalfe, Earl (Actor)
Meyer, Monica (Not known)
Millan, Sergio (Grocer)
Mitchell, Alex (Not known)
Mirro, Roger Joseph (Not known)
Moliere (Playwright)
Moody, Jerome (Not known)

Morrow, Victor (Actor)
Murillo-Moncada, Larry Ely

Nikaidoh, Hitoshi Christopher (Doctor)

O'Brien, Daniel John
O'Connor, Harry (Stuntman)
Otis Jr, James (Lawyer)

Parsons, Gram (Singer)
Phyall, David (Not known)
Pinkerton, Allan (Detective)

Quinn, Philip (Not known)

Randall, Jack (Actor)
Reichelt, Franz (Inventor)
Rhoads, Randy (Guitarist)

Sagal, Boris (Director)
Sky, Adam (DJ)
Staininger, Hans (Burgomaster)

Streeter, Bradley (Not known)
Stewart, Payne (Golfer)
Subramanian, Ravi (Aircraft Engineer)

Taylor, Henry (Pall Bearer)
Thomas, Olive (Actress)
Thomas, Paul G (Businessman)

Unknown (Not known)
Unknown (Construction worker)
Unknown (Not Known)

Vallandigham, Clement Laird (Lawyer)
Van Gogh, Vincent (Post-impressionist Painter)
Vatel, Francois (Majordomo)

Weldens, Barbara (Singer)
Wertheim, Dick (Tennis linesman)
Whinfrey, Stephen (Not known)
Williams, Robert (Assembly worker)
Williams, Tennessee (Playwright)
Woolf, Ben (Actor)

Yelchin, Anton (Actor)

A

**Ace, Johnny
(Alexander, John Marshall)**

Born | 09th June 1929

Died | 25th December 1954 (25)

Profession | Rhythm and Blues Singer.

Remembered for | My Song (Song). Never Let Me Go (Song). Pledging My Love (Song).

Cause of Death | Gunshot wound(s) (Accidental).

Details

During a break between shows at the City Auditorium in Houston, Ace was playing with a revolver and pointed it at his head, stating that it was not loaded. He then fired the gun, which was actually loaded, shooting himself in the side of his head.

Final Resting Place | New Park Cemetery, Memphis, Tennessee.

Aeschylus

Born | c. 524BCE

Died | c. 455BCE (69)

Profession | Playwright.

Remembered for | Being described as 'the father of tragedy'. The Persians (Play).

Cause of Death | Injuries sustained when struck by falling tortoise.

Details

It is said that Aeschylus died when an eagle dropped a tortoise on his head. The bird is said to have mistaken his baldhead for a rock and tried to use it to crack open the shell of the tortoise. According to Pliny the Elder (Roman author) he had been staying outside all day to ensure a prophecy that he would be killed 'by the fall of a house' did not come true. Scholars consider these events ludicrous, instead suggesting that they were fabricated by an unknown comic writer.

Final Resting Place | Unknown.

Allman, Duanne
(Allman, Howard Duane)

Born | 20th November 1946

Died | 29th October 1971 (24)

Profession | Guitarist.

Remembered for | Being the founder member of the Allman Brothers Band. Session musician with King Curtis, Aretha Franklin, Boz Scaggs, and Wilson Pickett.

Cause of Death | Injuries sustained in a motorcycle crash.

Details

While Allman was riding his motorcycle at high speed a truck, carrying a lumber crane stopped suddenly on the intersection forcing him to swerve sharply.

He collided with the truck and was thrown from his motorcycle, which landed on top of him and slid for 90 feet pinned beneath it, crushing his internal organs. He died in hospital several hours later due to internal injuries.

Final Resting Place | Rose Hill Cemetery, Macon, Georgia.

**Allport, Christopher
(Allport, Alexander Wise)**

Born | 17th June 1947

Died | 25th January 2008 (60)

Profession | Actor.

Remembered for | Jack Frost and Jack Frost 2 (Movies). Garden Party (Movie). Queen (Movie). Felicity (TV show). The Young and the Restless (TV show).

Cause of Death | Injuries sustained in an avalanche.

Details

Allport was one of three people killed when they were struck by three avalanches near the Mountain High Ski Resort in Wrightwood, San Bernardo County, California (in the San Gabriel Mountains). His body was recovered the following day.

Final Resting Place | Prospect Hill Cemetery, Nantucket, Massachusetts.

Amundsen, Roald (Amundsen, Robert Englebregt Gravning)

Born | 16th July 1872

Died | c. 18th June 1928 (55)

Profession | Explorer.

Remembered for | Leading the first expeditions to cross the Northwest Passage and reach the North and South Poles.

Cause of Death | Injuries sustained in a plane crash.

Details

Amundsen disappeared while taking part in a rescue mission onboard a flying boat to find the airship "Italia" which was stranded in the Arctic.

The aircraft was thought to have crashed in fog in the Barents Sea. A search mounted by the Norwegian Government was called of after three months. Amundsen's and the five other crew members bodies were never found.

Final Resting Place | Barents Sea.

Anderson, Sherwood

Born | 13th September 1876

Died | 08th March 1941 (64)

Profession | Author.

Remembered for | Dark Laughter (Novel) and the short story collections titled "Winesburgh, Ohio".

Cause of Death | Peritonitis (an infection of the inner lining of the stomach).

Details

Anderson accidentally swallowed a toothpick while drinking a cocktail on the cruise ship Santa Lucia that later caused fatal internal damage.

Final Resting Place | Round Hill Cemetery, Marion, Virginia.

Andrews, Thomas

Born | 07th February 1873

Died | 15th April 1912 (39)

Profession | Businessman and Shipbuilder.

Remembered for | Being the chief designer for the RMS Titanic.

Cause of Death | Died in the sinking of the RMS Titanic.

Details

Following the Titanic striking an iceberg and beginning to sink, Andrews was seen helping woman and children into lifeboats and throwing deckchairs and other floating objects to people in the water.

Final Resting Place | Atlantic Ocean (if recovered his body was never identified).

Arkeen, (Aaron) West

Born | 18th June 1960

Died | 30th May 1997 (36)

Profession | Musician and Songwriter.

Remembered for | (although he was never a member) co-writing several songs with Axl Rose for Guns N' Roses (Group). It's So Easy (Song). The Garden (Song). Yesterdays (Song).

Cause of Death | Drug overdose (Accidental).

Details

Arkeen was found dead in his Los Angeles home while he was recovering from severe burns he had sustained when an indoor barbeque had exploded. His death was ruled an "accidental opiate overdose".

Final Resting Place | Unknown.

B

Ballard, Florence (Glenda)

Born | 30th June 1943

Died | 22nd February 1976 (32)

Profession | Singer.

Remembered for | Being a member of The Supremes (Group). Singing on ten of their number one records. Baby Love (Song). Stop in the Name of Love (Song).

Cause of Death | Heart attack.

Details

Following being removed from The Supremes and an unsuccessful solo career Ballard, who struggled with alcoholism, depression and poverty, attended Mount Carmel Mercy Hospital in Detroit on the 21st of February complaining of numbness in her limbs. She died the next morning from a cardiac arrest caused by a blood clot in one of her arteries.

Final Resting Place | Detroit Memorial Park Cemetery, Warren, Michigan.

Ballard, Sam

Born | 10th May 1989

Died | 02nd October 2018 (29)

Profession | Rugby Player.

Remembered for | Not applicable.

Cause of Death | Eosinophilic Meningoencephaltitis (Meningitis).

Details

While at a party in 2010, Ballard ate a slug as a dare unaware that it was infected with rat lungworm. He immediately became ill and complained of serious pains in his legs. He had contracted Eosinophilic Meningoencephaltitis, which many people will recover from, but he fell into a coma for 420 days and when he finally awoke, he had a brain injury. Left severely disabled he struggled for the rest of his life trying to learn to walk and move his limbs again. He could not eat for himself and needed help going to the bathroom.

On 02nd August 2018, he became seriously ill and two months later died in Hornsby Hospital, Sydney.

Final Resting Place | Private.

Belk, Lottie Michelle

Born | 19th June 1960

Died | 08th June 2016 (55)

Profession | Not known.

Remembered for | Not applicable.

Cause of Death | Penetrating blunt force chest trauma.

Details

Belk died when a gust of wind caused an anchored umbrella to break free and blow across the beach stabbing her in the chest at Virginia Beach, Virginia. Conditions at the time were reported as winds gusting at 20 to 25mph. The Chief Medical Examiner later reported Belk's death as penetrating blunt force chest trauma adding that her death was accidental.

Final Resting Place | Wilkerson Memorial Cemetery, Petersburg, Petersburg City, Virginia, USA.

Bernecker, John

Born | 02nd March 1984

Died | 13th July 2017 (33)

Profession | Stuntman.

Remembered for | Olympus Has Fallen (Movie). The Hunger Games (Movie).

Cause of Death | Injuries sustained in a fall from height (Accidental).

Details

While performing a stunt for the TV show The Walking Dead, Bernecker fell 20 feet onto a concrete floor. He was said to have missed the safety cushion by "inches". He was placed on life support at the Atlanta Medical Center but died the next day from his injuries.

Final Resting Place | Metairie Cemetery, New Orleans, Louisiana.

Betts, James

Born | Unknown

Died | c. 1667 (?)

Profession | Student.

Remembered for | Not applicable.

Cause of Death | Asphyxiation.

Details

Betts was sealed in a cupboard at Corpus Christ College, Cambridge, UK by his lover Elizabeth Spencer in an attempt to hide him from her father, Doctor John Spencer, a priest and master of the college, who had unexpectedly returned to their quarters. Betts was trapped inside unaware that the cupboard could only be opened by a hidden spring on the outside.

It is thought that Spencer may have known he was in the cupboard as he ordered Elizabeth to immediately pack her belongings and she then departed with him on a long trip away from Cambridge. Consumed by grief Elizabeth Spencer committed suicide about a year later.

Final Resting Place |.

Biaksangzula, Peter

Born | 12th September 1991

Died | 19th October 2014 (23)

Profession | Footballer.

Remembered for | Midfielder for Bethlehem Vengthlang FC.

Cause of Death | Spinal Cord injury.

Details

Following a goal against Chanmari West, Biaksangzula suffered damage to his spine after attempting a celebratory somersault. Five days later despite emergency surgery and treatment in intensive care he died.

Final Resting Place | Unknown.

Biggs, Gregory Glenn

Born | 16th August 1964

Died | 26th October 2001 (37)

Profession | Not known.

Remembered for | Not applicable.

Cause of Death | Exsanguination (Bleeding out).

Details

Chante Jawan Mallard (25), who was on her way home, hit Biggs with her car. Although he did not suffer fatal injuries his head and shoulders became lodged in the windscreen. He died later after Mallard left her car in the garage with Biggs still stuck in the windscreen and he bled to death. Mallard was found guilty of murder and sentenced to 60 years in prison.

Final Resting Place | Crown Hill Memorial Park, Dallas, Texas.

Bonham, John Henry

Born | 31st May 1948

Died | 25th September 1980 (32)

Profession | Drummer and Songwriter.

Remembered for | Being regarded by many as the greatest and most influential drummer of all time. Led Zeppelin (Group).

Cause of Death | Pulmonary Aspiration.

Details

The inquest into Bonham's death revealed that he had drunk the equivalent of one to 1.4 litres of 40% ABV vodka after which he vomited and choked to death. The finding was accidental death.

Final Resting Place | Rushock Parish Church, Worcestershire.

Bowman, Mildred

Born | c. 1943

Died | c. 01st August 2005 (62)

Profession | Not known.

Remembered for | Not applicable.

Cause of Death | Suffocation.

Details

Bowman and her sister Alice Wardle (68), on holiday in Benidorm, Spain, died by suffocation when they became trapped in their fold-up Murphy bed which had collapsed on top of them while they were asleep. The Coroner at the inquest in Gateshead said that the deaths could have been avoided if the bed had been correctly fitted to the wall.

Final Resting Place | Unknown.

Brahe, Tycho
(Brahe, Tyge Ottesen)

Born | 14th December 1546

Died | 24th October 1601 (54)

Profession | Astronomer, Astrologer and Alchemist.

Remembered for | His observations on mapping the night sky.

Cause of Death | Bladder ailment.

Details

While attending a banquet in Prague, Brahe refused to leave the table to relieve himself as he considered it would have been a breach of etiquette. After drinking too much his bladder burst. He died in agony eleven days later from a bladder infection. He wrote his own epitaph "He lived like a sage and died like a fool".

Final Resting Place | Church of Our Lady before Tyn, Old Town of Prague.

Brenno, Jeremy T "Geoff"

Born | 10th April 1978

Died | 09th July 1994 (16)

Profession | Not known.

Remembered for | Not applicable.

Cause of Death | Exsanguination (Bleeding out).

Details

While playing golf with friends at the Kingsboro Golf Club, after a bad shot, Brenno slammed his No3 wooden golf club against a bench. The shaft broke and bounced back piercing his Pulmonary Vein.

Final Resting Place | Unknown.

Brohm, Francis Daniel

Born | 03rd November 1981

Died | 29th August 2004 (22)

Profession | Not known.

Remembered for | Not applicable.

Cause of Death | Decapitation.

Details

While being driven home in a pickup truck by his friend John Kemper Hutcherson (21) in Marietta, Cobb County, Kentucky as Brohm was hanging out the passenger window Hutcherson swerved off the road and hit a telephone support wire side-on. The collision resulted in Brohm being decapitated. Hutcherson drove for another twelve miles to his home in Atlanta, Georgia then parked up in his driveway and went to bed in his blood soaked clothes. A neighbour found Brohm's headless body in the truck the next morning. Brohm's severed head was recovered from the accident site. Hutcherson was charged with 'vehicular homicide and DUI'.

Final Resting Place | Cavalry Cemetery, Louisville, Jefferson County, Kentucky, USA.

Brown, Basil

Born | c. 1926

Died | c. February 1974 (48)

Profession | Health Food Enthusiast.

Remembered for | Not applicable.

Cause of Death | Liver failure.

Details

Brown died from liver damage after consuming 70 million units of Vitamin A and 10 gallons (38 litres) of carrot juice over a period of ten days.

When he died his skin had turned bright yellow. The pathologist who performed the autopsy said that the effect of an enormous intake of Vitamin A was indistinguishable from alcoholic poisoning and will produce the same result: mainly cirrhosis of the liver.

Final Resting Place | Unknown.

**Buckley, Jeff
(Moorhead, Scott)**

Born | 17th November 1966

Died | 29th May 1997 (30)

Profession | Singer. Songwriter. Guitarist.

Remembered for | Grace (Album). Dream Brother (Song). Eternal Life (Song). Hallelujah (Song –cover).

Cause of Death | Drowning (Accidental).

Details

During the evening of 29th May, Buckley went swimming in Wolf River Harbour, a water channel of the Mississippi River, wearing all his clothing and boots while singing the chorus of the Led Zeppelin song "Whole Lotta Love". A roadie, Keith Foti, remained onshore. After a tug boat passed Foti could no longer see Buckley. Despite an extensive search that night and the following day his body was not found until the 04th June. The autopsy report stated that there were no drugs or alcohol in his system and he was in good spirits before his disappearance. His death was ruled to be accidental drowning.

Final Resting Place | Cremated, but there is a Memorial to Buckley at Memphis Zoo, Memphis, Shelby County, Tennessee.

~30~

Budlong, Jack

Born | 22nd February 1913

Died | 05th August 1941 (28)

Profession | Polo player and Movie extra.

Remembered for | Not applicable.

Cause of Death | Peritonitis (an infection of the inner lining of the stomach).

Details

On the 25th June 1941, while filming on the set of "They Died With Their Boots On" (Movie) in Calabasas, Los Angeles, Budlong (a skilled horseman) had to do a high-speed ride while holding a sabre. For some unknown reason Budlong insisted on using a real sabre rather than a wooden prop.

During the scene the horse became spooked and reared up. Budlong threw the sabre away before the horse fell on him but it landed with the blade facing upward and impaled him in the abdomen and back. He died six weeks later in hospital.

Final Resting Place | Forest Lawn Memorial Park, Glendale, California.

Burduchenko, Inna (Georgiyevna)

Born | 31st March 1939

Died | 15th August 1960 (21)

Profession | Actress.

Remembered for | Ivanna (Movie). Flower on the Stoned (Movie).

Cause of Death | Third-degree burns.

Details

While Burduchenko was filming in a burning barn for the movie "Tsvetok na Kamne" in Donetsk, Ukraine part of the roof fell on her. She suffered 78% burns to her body and died two weeks later.

Final Resting Place | Baikove Cemetery, Keiv, Ukraine.

Burger, Rebecca

Born | 1984

Died | 18th June 2017 (33)

Profession | Fitness blogger. Model.

Remembered for | Not applicable.

Cause of Death | Heart attack.

Details

Burger died following what was termed a "domestic accident" after a whipped cream dispenser exploded and struck her in the chest triggering a heart attack. The incident occurred on 17th June and she died the following day.

Final Resting Place | Unknown.

Burrus, Joseph "Amazing Joe"

Born | c. 1958

Died | 31st October 1990 (32)

Profession | Magician, Illusionist and Escape Artist.

Remembered for | Not applicable.

Cause of Death | Asphyxiation (Accidental).

Details

Burrus was performing one of his escape routines at Blackbeard's Family Fun Centre in Fresno, California. This involved him being placed in a plastic coffin, chained and handcuffed, then put into a seven feet deep grave, and seven tons of dirt and wet concrete poured on top of the coffin. The weight of the dirt and concrete caused the coffin to collapse crushing and burying him alive. His death was seen by hundreds of onlookers, including his children, while it was being shown on a large video screen and broadcast live on the radio. He had successful performed the same stunt a year earlier but had only used dirt. He had not calculated the weight of the dirt and concrete combined.

Final Resting Place | Unknown.

Burton, Cliff (Clifford Lee)

Born | 10th February 1962

Died | 27th September 1986 (24)

Profession | Musician and Songwriter.

Remembered for | Metallica (Bass player).

Cause of Death | Injuries sustained in a bus crash.

Details

Around 19:00 the bus Metallica were travelling on from Stockholm to Copenhagen, according to the driver, ran over a patch of black ice near the village of Dorarp and fell into a ditch. As it continued to roll over Burton was thrown out a window and landed beneath the bus.

Everyone else on the bus escaped with minor injuries. The cause of the accident was never truly established.

Final Resting Place | Ashes scattered in San Francisco Bay.

C

**Castle, Vernon
(Blyth, William Vernon)**

Born | 02nd May 1887

Died | 15th February 1918 (30)

Profession | Ballroom dancer.

Remembered for | Being credited with reviving the popularity of modern dancing. Starring in Irvine Berlin's Broadway show "Watch Your Step".

Cause of Death | Injuries sustained in a plane crash.

Details

After taking off from Benbrook Field, near Fort Worth, at only 70 feet, Castle had to make a sharp turn to avoid a collision with another plane. He was thrown out of his plane, which had stalled, and fell 45 feet; the plane then went out of control and crashed. He was the only fatality. The other pilot, a student cadet, and Castle's pet Monkey "Jeffrey" sustained minor injuries.

Final Resting Place | Woodlawn Cemetery Bronx, Bronx County, New York.

Chaibancha, Mitr

Born | 28th January 1934

Died | 08th October 1970 (36)

Profession | Actor and Stuntman.

Remembered for | Appearing in 266 movies. Operation Bangkok (Movie). Insee Thong (Golden Eagle) (Movie).

Cause of Death | Injuries sustained in a fall from height (Accidental).

Details

Chaibancha was filming a stunt for the final scene of "Insee Thong" (Movie) which involved him grabbing a rope ladder hanging beneath a helicopter and flying off into the distance.

When he went to grab the ladder he only managed to reach the first rung. Unaware of this the helicopter pilot continued to climb. Chaibancha lost his grip and fell 300 feet to the ground. His death was ruled an accident.

Final Resting Place | Cremated.

Chaney, Lon (Leonidas Frank)

Born | 01st April 1883

Died | 26th August 1930 (47)

Profession | Actor

Remembered for | The Hunchback of Notre Dame (Movie). The Phantom of the Opera (Movie).

Cause of Death | Laryngeal cancer.

Details

In the winter of 1929 during the filming of "Thunder" Chaney developed pneumonia. Later that year he was diagnosed with bronchial lung cancer, which was aggravated by the artificial snow, made from cornflakes becoming logged in his throat during filming. This caused a serious infection and his condition quickly deteriorated resulting in him dying from a throat haemorrhage.

Final Resting Place | Forest Lawn Memorial Park, Glendale, California.

Charondas

Born | Unknown

Died | c. 7th to 5th BCE

Profession | Lawgiver.

Remembered for | Not applicable.

Cause of Death | Injuries sustained by self-inflicted sword wounds.

Details

Charondas was a Greek lawgiver in Catania, Italy who passed a law that stated the punishment for anyone who brought weapons into the public Assembly was death. One day he arrived at the Assembly with a sword attached to his belt. In order to uphold his own law he immediately committed suicide.

Final Resting Place | Unknown.

Cooke, Sam

Born | 22nd January 1931

Died | 11th December 1964 (33)

Profession | Singer and Songwriter.

Remembered for | Wonderful World (Song). Chain Gang (Song) Twistin' The Night Away (Song).

Cause of Death | Gunshot wound(s) (Justifiable killing).

Details

Cooke was shot and killed by Bertha Franklin the Manager of the Hacienda Motel, Los Angeles. Franklin stated that she had shot Cooke in self-defence after he had broken into her office and attacked her. A court later ruled that his death was justifiable homicide, which Cooke's family and friends have always disputed.

Final Resting Place | Forest Lawn Memorial Park, Glendale, California.

**Cooper, Tommy
(Cooper, Thomas Frederick)**

Born | 19th March 1921

Died | 15th April 1984 (63)

Profession | Comedian and Magician.

Remembered for | The Tommy Cooper Hour (TV show). Cooper's Half Hour (TV show). Cooper: Just Like That (TV show).

Cause of Death | Heart attack.

Details

Cooper collapsed and died on the live LWT TV show "Live From Her Majesty's" broadcast from Her Majesty's Theatre in Westminster. As he fell backwards gasping for air the audience, thinking it was part of his act, laughed loudly. The show continued once Cooper had being pulled back through the stage curtains.

Final Resting Place | Cremated.

Croce, Jim
(Croce, James Joseph)

Born | 10th January 1943

Died | 20th September 1973 (30)

Profession | Singer and Songwriter.

Remembered for | Time in a Bottle (Song). Bad Bad Leroy Brown (Song). You Don't Mess Around With Jim (Album).

Cause of Death | Injuries sustained in a plane crash.

Details

Croce, along with five others, boarded a chartered Beechcraft E18S at Natchitoches Regional Airport, Louisiana. During take-off the aircraft crashed into a tree at the end of the runway killing all on board. An investigation showed that the pilot had failed to gain sufficient altitude to clear the tree, and even though it was the only tree in the area and a clear night, he had not tried to avoid it.

Final Resting Place | Haym Salomon Memorial Park, Frazer, Pennsylvania.

Cummings, John

Born | c. 1886

Died | c. March 1809 (23)

Profession | Sailor.

Remembered for | Not applicable.

Cause of Death | Internal injuries caused by swallowing various metal objects.

Details

After watching a circus knife-swallower while on shore leave in France Cummings began swallowing knives. It is said that on one occasion he swallowed four knives and quickly passed three, suffering no ill effects. in 1805, after managing to successfully pass fourteen knives with only minor abdominal pain he swallowed twenty knives and a case.

He only managed to pass the case and four years later as his health deteriorated, and now under the care of a Doctor Curry he died at Guy's hospital in London, UK. His autopsy revealed that his intestines were full of black iron oxide and pieces of metal. In addition, 30 to 40 pieces of razor shard were found in his stomach.

Final Resting Place | Unknown.

D

Daniel, Jack
(Daniel, Jasper Newton)

Born | 05th September 1850

Died | 10th October 1911 (61)

Profession | Distiller and Businessman.

Remembered for | Being the founder of the Jack Daniels Tennessee Whisky distillery.

Cause of Death | Blood poisoning.

Details

The tale of his death which is often told, but proclaimed by his biographer to not be true, is that Daniel's died after an infection started in one of his toes. This was said to have happened when he kicked his safe in anger, as he could not get it to open. He was said to have always had issues recalling the combination.

Final Resting Place | Lynchburg City Cemetery, Lynchburg, Tennessee.

Di Paolo, Renato

Born | c. 1977

Died | 22nd April 2000 (23)

Profession | Actor.

Remembered for | Not applicable.

Cause of Death | Asphyxiation (Accidental).

Details

Di Paolo was playing the part of Judas Iscariot in a re-enactment of the play "Way of the Cross" in the village of Camerata Nuova, Lazio in Italy. The final scene required him to be tied to a tree by a noose and jump off a rock about a foot from the ground, something that he had safely done the previous evening. However, this time when he jumped the noose tightened around his neck and strangled him. He was taken to hospital where he was pronounced dead. In the audience were Di Paolo's parents.

Final Resting Place | Unknown.

Didenko, Valenti

Born | c. 1988

Died | 29th February 2020 (32)

Profession | Not Known.

Remembered for | Not Known.

Cause of Death | Suffocation.

Details

Didenko was one of three people who died (the others were Yury Alferov and Natalia Monakova, both 25) when 25kg (55lb) of dry ice was thrown into an indoor swimming pool at a party to celebrate the 29th birthday of a blogger Ekaterina Didenko in a sauna and pool complex in Moscow.

The Carbon Dioxide from the dry ice displaced the oxygen resulting in the three victims dying from Carbon Dioxide suffocation and drowning. Four others suffered chemical burns and poisoning. Didenko, whose husband was one of the victims, had intended to impress her guests by creating a dramatic fog-cloud visual effect.

Final Resting Place | Unknown.

Disi, Salvatore ("Sal")

Born | 16th April 1956

Died | 10th January 2019 (62)

Profession | Pilot.

Remembered for | Not Known.

Cause of Death | Decapitation (Accidental).

Details

Disi was decapitated while using a power cart to start a Bell 230 helicopter at Brooksville-Tampa Bay Regional Airport. An unexpected up and down movement of the helicopter caused the main rotor blades to strike Disi.

Final Resting Place | Unknown.

Draco (Dracon) of Athens

Born | Unknown

Died | c. 600BCE

Profession | Lawgiver.

Remembered for | His harshness when handing out punishments which lead to the term 'draconian' now being used to refer to unforgiving laws.

Cause of Death | Suffocation.

Details

Draco, an Athenian lawgiver, died in the Aeginetan theatre, Aegina, Greece when his supporters, in a traditional ancient Greek show of approval, threw their coats, shirts, and hats over him. There were so many items thrown over his head that he suffocated.

Final Resting Place | Unknown.

Driscoll, Bobby
(Driscoll, Robert Clets)

Born | 03rd March 1937

Died | 30th March 1968 (31)

Profession | Actor.

Remembered for | Song of the South (Movie). Peter Pan (Movie). Treasure Island (Movie). The Window (Movie).

Cause of Death | Heart failure.

Details

When his career started to decline Driscoll became addicted to drugs and was even sent to prison for illicit drug use.

After his release, in ill health due to his substance abuse and having no money left, he stayed in an abandoned East Village tenement in Manhattan. His body was found lying in a cot with empty beer bottles and religious pamphlets lying around him. The medical examiner determined that he had died from heart failure due to hardening of the arteries caused by long term drug abuse. His body went unclaimed and he was buried in an unmarked pauper's grave. 19 months after his death his mother sought the help of the New York Police to try to trace him as his father was close to death. This resulted in a fingerprint match, which located his resting place on Hart Island where he remains buried.

Final Resting Place | Potter's Field, Hart Island, New York.

Duncan, (Angela) Isadora

Born | 26th May 1877

Died | 14th September 1927 (50)

Profession | Dancer.

Remembered for | Being known as the "Modern Mother of Dance". Performing to acclamation across America, Russia and Europe.

Cause of Death | Strangulation (Accidental).

Details

Duncan was a passenger in a car on the Promenade Des Anglais, Nice, France being driven by Benoit Falchetto.

As they set off the long flowing silk scarf she was wearing around her neck became tangled around the car's open spoke wheels and rear axle pulling her from the car, breaking her neck and her spine in two places. She died instantly.

Final Resting Place | Pere Lachaise Cemetery, Paris, France.

E

Earhart, Amelia (Mary)

Born | 24th July 1897

Died | Disappeared 02nd July 1937 (39)

Profession | Pilot.

Remembered for | Aviation Pioneer. Being the first female to fly solo across the Atlantic Ocean.

Cause of Death | Not known.

Details

While on an expedition to circumnavigate the globe in a Purdue University funded twin-engine Lockheed Model 10E Electra (NR16020) Earhart, and her navigator Fred Noonan, disappeared en route from Lae to Howland Island in the Pacific Ocean. She was declared legally dead on 05th January 1939.

Final Resting Place | Unknown.

Edwards, Mike

Born | 31st May 1948

Died | 03rd September 2010 (62)

Profession | Cellist and Music Teacher.

Remembered for | Being a member of the Electric Light Orchestra (Group)

Cause of Death | Injuries sustained in a car crash.

Details

Edwards died on the A381 road between Harbertonford and Halwell when a 590kg hay bale rolled down a hillside and collided with his van. Two defendants charged in relation to the accident were found not guilty.

Final Resting Place | Bidwell Woodland Natural Burial Ground, Rattery, South Hampshire, Devon.

Edwards, Richey (Richard James)

Born | 22nd December 1967

Died | disappeared 01st February 1995 (27)

Profession | Guitarist and Songwriter.

Remembered for | Maniac Street Preachers (Group). Lyrics for all the songs on Journal for Plague (Album released 18th May 2009).

Cause of Death | Not known.

Details

The day Edwards was due to fly out of Britain for an American promotional tour he disappeared. He was legally declared dead on 23rd November 2008.

Final Resting Place | Unknown.

Entwistle, (Lillian Millicent) Peg

Born | 05th February 1908

Died | 16th September 1932 (24)

Profession | Actress.

Remembered for | Thirteen Women (Movie). The Man From Toronto (Stage play). Little Women (Stage play).

Cause of Death | Injuries sustained in a fall from height (Suicide).

Details

Entwistle climbed a workman's ladder to the top of the "H" on the Hollywood sign and jumped. She died from multiple fractures of the pelvis and internal injuries.

Final Resting Place | Oak Hill Cemetery, Springdale, Ohio.

F

Findlay, Michael

Born | 27th August 1937

Died | 16th May 1977 (39)

Profession | Filmmaker, Producer and Screenwriter.

Remembered for | Snuff (Movie). The Touch of Her Flesh (Movie).

Cause of Death | Decapitation (Accidental).

Details

Along with 21 other passengers Findlay was waiting to board a Sikorsky S-61 helicopter on top of the Pan-Am Building in New York when the helicopters landing gear failed and it tipped over onto its side. Findlay and two other passengers were slashed and decapitated by the detaching spinning rotor blades. Another passenger died later in hospital and a woman on the ground was killed by falling debris.

Final Resting Place | Unknown.

G

Garcia, Joana Sainz

Born | c. 1989

Died | 01st September 2019 (30)

Profession | Singer, Songwriter and Dancer.

Remembered for | Performing with the Orquesta Super Hollywood for six years.

Cause of Death | Injuries sustained when struck by pyrotechnic.

Details

Garcia was struck in the abdomen and knocked unconscious by shards of metal from an exploding pyrotechnic while performing with the Super Hollywood Orchestra at a concert at Las Berlanas in Madrid. She died later in hospital. The group's promoter said that they had been performing the same act for five years without any incidents.

Final Resting Place | Unknown.

Gingrich, Greg Austin

Born | 11th October 1954

Died | 28th November 1992 (38)

Profession | Not known.

Remembered for | Not applicable.

Cause of Death | Injuries sustained in a fall from height (Accidental).

Details

Gingrich jumped onto rock wall on the "Rim Trail" near El Tovar in the Grand Canyon, Coconino County, Arizona. He started to windmill his arms pretending to lose his balance to scare his teenage daughter. He then "fell" off the wall on the canyon side onto a small slope where he thought he could safely land. However, Gingrich missed his footing and fell 400 feet to his death.

Final Resting Place | Sparkman Hillcrest Memorial Park, Dallas, Dallas County, Texas.

Glynn, Molly

Born | 14th June 1968

Died | 06th September 2014 (46)

Profession | Actress.

Remembered for | Chicago Fire (TV show).

Cause of Death | Injuries sustained when struck by a falling tree.

Details

On the 05th September Glynn and her husband, Joe Foust, were cycling on the North Branch Trail in Erickson Woods (a suburb of Chicago) when a sudden storm caused wind gusts of over 70mph. As they tried to take shelter a tree fell on them. Although Foust was not badly injured Glynn died the next day in hospital.

Final Resting Place | Unknown.

Godel, Kurt Friedrich

Born | 28th April 1906

Died | 14th January 1978 (71)

Profession | Mathematician, Philosopher and Logician.

Remembered for | Being considered one of the most significant Logicians in history.

Cause of Death | Malnutrition and Inanition (exhaustion caused by lack of nourishment) caused by personality disturbance.

Details

Godel suffered later in his life from Mental Insatiability and developed an obsessive fear of being poisoned. He would only eat food prepared by his wife and when she was hospitalised for six months he refused to eat. He eventually starved to death and weighted only 65lb when he died.

Final Resting Place | Princeton Cemetery, Princeton, New Jersey.

Grundman, David

Born | 1957

Died | 1982 (25)

Profession | Not known.

Remembered for | Saguaro (Song) being written about him by The Austin Lounge Lizards.

Cause of Death | Injuries sustained when struck by a falling Saguaro Cactus.

Details

While Grundman was shooting at Cacti near Lake Pleasant in Arizona a four foot length of limb weighing 500lb detached and fell crushing him. The trunk of the Cactus then also fell on him.

Final Resting Place | Riverhurst Cemetery, Endwell, Broome, New York.

H

Harron, Robert Emmett

Born | 12th April 1893

Died | 05th September 1920 (27)

Profession | Actor.

Remembered for | The Birth of a Nation (Movie). Intolerance (Movie).

Cause of Death | Gunshot wound(s) (Accidental).

Details

On 01st September Harron checked into the Hotel Seymour in Wisconsin with his friend, screenwriter and director Victor Heerman, who he was sharing a room with. After attending a poorly received preview of his film "Coincidence" he returned alone to his room. At some point Harron sustained a gunshot wound to his chest. According to Harron himself, as he was taking clothes from his trunk a gun wrapped in his trousers fell and fired a shot into his chest puncturing his lung. Harron phoned for help and apparently joked with the Hotel Manager that he was in "A Devil of a fix, having shot himself". He was taken to Bellevue Hospital Center where he died four days later from his wounds.

Final Resting Place | Calvary Cemetery, Queens, New York.

Harvey, Leslie Cameron

Born | 13th September 1944

Died | 03rd May 1972 (27)

Profession | Guitarist.

Remembered for | Being the co-founder and lead guitarist of Stone the Crows (Group). Fool on the Hill (Song). Raining in Your Heart (Song). Danger Zone (Song).

Cause of Death | Electrocution (Accidental).

Details

While performing at the Top Rank Ballroom in Swansea, Harvey (brother of Alex Harvey) was electrocuted after touching a microphone that was not earth-grounded.

Final Resting Place | Unknown.

Hayes, Frank

Born | c. 1901

Died | 04th June 1923 (22)

Profession | Horse trainer.

Remembered for | Not applicable.

Cause of Death | Heart attack.

Details

Hayes died of a heart attack mid-race at Belmont Park racetrack, Elmont, Nassau County, New York, USA. He collapsed but stayed on his horse (Sweet Kiss) which crossed the finish line in first place. Although a horse trainer, this was his first race as a jockey.

Out of respect, the result was uncontested and Belmont's jockey club declared him the winner. His horse never raced again and was said to have been renamed 'The Sweet Kiss of Death'.

Final Resting Place | Holy Cross Cemetery, Brooklyn, Kings County, New York, USA.

Hernandez, Humberto

Born | c. 1983

Died | 21st June 2007 (24)

Profession | Not known.

Remembered for | Not applicable.

Cause of Death | Injuries sustained when struck by an airborne fire hydrant.

Details

While walking with his wife in Oakland, California, Hernandez was killed when he was hit on the back of the head by a 200lb fire hydrant that the water pressure had fired into the air after being struck by an SUV. The Police report recorded that if he had been one step behind or one step ahead the hydrant would have missed him.

Final Resting Place | Unknown.

Herzberg, Elaine

Born | 02nd August 1968

Died | 18th March 2018 (49)

Profession | Not applicable.

Remembered for | Being the first person to die after being hit by a self-driving (autonomous) car.

Cause of Death | Injuries sustained when struck by a car.

Details

As Herzberg pushed her bicycle across a four-lane road in Tempe, Arizona she was struck by an Uber test vehicle. After the accident Uber suspended testing of self-drive vehicles in Arizona.

Final Resting Place | Resthaven Park East Cemetery, Phoenix, Maricopa County, Arizona.

Heselden, Jimi (James William)

Born | 27th March 1948

Died | 26th September 2010 (62)

Profession | Entrepreneur.

Remembered for | Being the owner of Segway Inc.

Cause of Death | Injuries sustained in a fall from height (Accidental).

Details

While driving his Segway vehicle along a cliff path above the village of Thorp Arch near Boston Spa, West Yorkshire, Heselden moved aside to allow a dog walker space to pass. In doing so he attempted to reverse and ended up falling 80 feet into the River Wharfe.

Final Resting Place | Unknown.

Hexum, Jon-Erik

Born | 05th November 1957

Died | 18th October 1984 (27)

Profession | Actor.

Remembered for | Voyagers! (TV show). Cover Up (TV show).

Cause of Death | Gunshot wound(s) (Accidental).

Details

On the 12th October while on the set of "Cover Up" where the crew were also filming Golden Opportunity (TV show), Hexum became impatient with the delay to him being filmed loading a .44 Magnum handgun, for which he had been provided blanks, and began playing around with the gun. He had unloaded it except for one blank round and began mimicking Russian Roulette. He put the gun to his right temple and pulled the trigger, apparently unaware that his actions were perilous. The force of the blank shattered a quarter of his skull causing pieces to be logged in his brain resulting in massive haemorrhaging. Six days after the accident he was declared dead and his body was flown to San Francisco on life-support where his mother agreed to donate his organs. His death was ruled to be accidental.

Final Resting Place | Cremated. Ashes scattered in the Pacific Ocean near Malibu, California.

Hiromi, Katsuki

Born | 21st August 1936

Died | 01st April 1958 (21)

Profession | Actress.

Remembered for | Not applicable.

Cause of Death | Bisection (Accidental).

Details

During a performance of "Spring Dance" at the Grand Theatre in Takarazuka, Japan, Hiromi's clothing was caught in the mechanism of a stage lift. Unable to free herself her feet were dragged into the moving mechanism and a metal band cut through her torso killing her instantly.

Final Resting Place | Unknown.

Houdini, Harry
(**Weisz, Erik** then **Weiss, Enrich** or **Weiss, Harry**)

Born | 24th March 1874

Died | 31st October 1926 (52)

Profession | Illusionist and Stunt performer.

Remembered for | Being one of the greatest magicians and escapists of all time. Being the exposer of fake spiritualists and fraudulent escape artists.

Cause of Death | Peritonitis.

Details

A McGill University student, Jocelyn Gordon Whitehead, was in Houdini's dressing room in the Princess Theatre in Montreal when he asked him whether it was true that punches in the stomach did not hurt him. Before Houdini replied Whitehead started to deliver hammer-like blows below his belt. Houdini, who was reclining on a coach, having broken his ankle several days early winced at each punch and gestured for Whitehead to stop, as he had no opportunity to prepare himself for such blows. Houdini was unable to sleep as he was in constant pain but did not seek medical help.

Two days later when he did visit a doctor he had a temperature of 39C and acute appendicitis. He was advised to have an immediate operation but ignored this advice and decided to go on with his show on the 24th October at the Garrick Theatre in Detroit, Michigan. Afterwards he was hospitalised at the Grace Hospital, Detroit. He died seven days later of Peritonitis secondary to a ruptured appendix.

Final Resting Place | Machpelah Cemetery, Glendale, New York.

Hoy, Gary

Born | 01st January 1955

Died | 09th July 1993 (38)

Profession | Lawyer.

Remembered for | Not applicable.

Cause of Death | Injuries sustained in a fall from height (Accidental).

Details

While attempting to prove to a group of prospective trainee lawyers that the windows in his office on the 24th floor in the Dominion Centre in Toronto were unbreakable, Hoy throw himself against the glass. While the glass did not break the whole window frame gave way and Hoy fell to his death.

Final Resting Place | Unknown.

I

Irwin, Steve

Born | 22nd February 1962

Died | 04th September 2006 (44)

Profession | Zookeeper, Conservationist and TV personality.

Remembered for | The Crocodile Hunter (TV show). Being the owner of Australia Zoo.

Cause of Death | Internal bleeding (Accidental).

Details

Irwin died while filming an underwater documentary "Ocean's Deadliest" at Batt Reef near Port Douglas, Queensland. When he was swimming in chest-deep water he approached a Short-tail Stingray (with a span of around two metres) from behind. The Stingray suddenly turned and started stabbing wildly with its tail. Irwin initially thought he had a punctured lung but a barb had pierced his heart and he bled to death,

Final Resting Place | Australia Zoo, Beerwah, Sunshine Coast Council, Queensland.

J

Johnson, Robert (Leroy)

Born | 08th May 1911

Died | 16th August 1938 (27)

Profession | Blues Singer, Guitarist and Songwriter.

Remembered for | The Complete Recordings (Album). King of the Delta Blues Singers (Album). Crossroads Blues (Song).

Cause of Death | Not known.

Details

Johnson was found by the side of the road near Greenwood, Mississippi. His death was not publicly reported at the time. Nearly 30 years later Gayle Dean Wardlow (a musicologist researcher) found his death certificate. It only recorded the date and location of his death.

Final Resting Place | Mount Zion Missionary Baptist Church, Morgan City, Mississippi.

Jordan, John

Born | 12th April 1925

Died | 16th May 1969 (44)

Profession | Cameraman.

Remembered for | His camera work on You Only Live Twice (Movie). Chitty Chitty Bang Bang (Movie).

Cause of Death | Injuries sustained in a fall from height (Accidental).

Details

In 1967, while filming "You Only Live Twice", Jordan was leaning out of a helicopter to get a better shot when another helicopter was caught by a gust of wind and was blown towards him. The rotor blade cut his leg, which later had to be amputated. In 1970 while filming "Catch 22" over the Gulf of Mexico in a Boeing B-25 Mitchell another plane passed close by and Jordan was sucked out the open door and fell 2,000 feet to his death. He had always refused to wear a safety harness.

Final Resting Place | Unknown.

𝒦

Kath, Terry (Alan)

Born | 31st January 1946

Died | 23rd January 1978 (33)

Profession | Musician and Songwriter.

Remembered for | Being the founding member of Chicago (Group). If You Leave Me Now (Song). Searchin' So Long (Song). Live In Japan (Album).

Cause of Death | Gunshot wound(s) (Accidental).

Details

After a party at the home of Roadie Don Johnson in Woodland Hills, Los Angeles, Kath began to play around with his guns. He picked up a semi-automatic 9mm pistol and leaning back in a chair said to Johnson who was warning him to be careful "Don't worry about it. Look the clip is not even in it". He then showed Johnson the empty magazine, which he put back in the gun. He put the gun to his temple and pulled the trigger unaware that there was a round in the chamber. He died instantly.

Final Resting Place | Forest Lawn Memorial Park, Glendale, California.

Keilberth, Joseph

Born | 19th April 1908

Died | 20th July 1968 (60)

Profession | Orchestral Conductor.

Remembered for | Being Principal Conductor of the Bavarian State Opera in Munich.

Cause of Death | Not known.

Details

While conducting the second act of Wagner's "Tristan and Isolde" in Munich, Keilberth collapsed and died in exactly the same place, that conductor Felix Motti had collapsed and died in 1911, while conducting the same opera.

A medical investigation carried out by Herbert von Karajan revealed that during rehearsals the conductor showed a massive increase in their stress levels.

Final Resting Place | Unknown.

Kivlenieks, Matiss Edmunds

Born | 26th August 1996

Died | 04th July 2021 (24)

Profession | Professional Ice Hockey Goaltender.

Remembered for | Playing for Prizma Riga, Cleveland Monsters and the Columbus Blue Jackets.

Cause of Death | Chest trauma.

Details

Kivlenieks had travelled to the home of the Blue Jackets goaltending coach Manny Legace in Novi, Michigan to celebrate Independence Day and the wedding of Legace's daughter. According to Novi Police fireworks, which included nine different tubes, were launched from a grassy area. The tubes tipped as the eighth shot was fired and the ninth shot hit Kivlenieks' on the chest. He was taken to Ascension Providence Hospital, suffering from extensive internal injuries, where he was subsequently pronounced dead. An autopsy ruled that Kivlenieks' death was accidental and due to a percussive injury caused by fireworks mortar blast, which caused major trauma to his heart and lungs. Columbus Blue Jackets goaltender Elvis Merzlikins called Kivlenieks a hero, saying that he saved him, his wife, and his unborn son.

Final Resting Place | Unknown.

L

Lam, Elisa

Born | 30th April 1991

Died | c. early February 2013 (21)

Profession | Student.

Remembered for | Not applicable.

Cause of Death | Drowning (Accidental).

Details

After being missing for several weeks, Lam was found dead in a large water tank on the roof of the Cecil Hotel in Los Angeles on the 19th February after guests had complained about the taste of the water.

The Coroner reported her cause of death as accidental drowning with bipolar disorder a significant factor.

Final Resting Place | Forest Lawn Memorial Park, Burnaby, Vancouver Regional District, British Columbia.

Larsson, Stig

Born | 15th August 1954

Died | 09th November 2004 (50)

Profession | Writer and Journalist.

Remembered for | Men Who Hate Women (Novel). The Girl Who Played With Fire (Novel). The Air Castle That Was Blown Up (Novel).

English translation by Reg Keelan under the titles 'The Girl with the Dragon Tattoo' 'The Girl Who Played with Fire' 'The Girl Who Kicked the Hornets Nest'.

Cause of Death | Heart attack.

Details

Larsson died of a heart attack while climbing the 197 stairs to his office due to the lift being out of order. He never exercised and his diet was said to consist almost entirely of cigarettes (60 a day), fast food, and large amounts of coffee.

Final Resting Place | Hogalid Church Cemetery, Sodermailm, Stockholm, Sweden.

Lazear, Jesse William

Born | 02nd May 1866

Died | 25th September 1900 (34)

Profession | Physician.

Remembered for | Confirming the hypothesis of Carlos Finlay that Mosquitoes transmitted Yellow Fever.

Cause of Death | Yellow fever.

Details

While in Cuba, Lazear was asked to join the yellow fever commission. As part of his research, he deliberately allowed an infected mosquito to bite him. Five days later, he was taken ill with yellow fever and four days after that he died.

Final Resting Place | Loudon Park Cemetery, Baltimore, Baltimore City, Maryland.

Leach, Bobby

Born | c. 1858

Died | 26th April 1926 (68)

Profession | Daredevil and stuntman.

Remembered for | Being the second person to go over Niagara Falls in a barrel (25th July 1911).

Cause of Death | Complications arising from Gangrene infection.

Details

Leach was a well-known stuntman and daredevil who performed with the Barnum and Bailey Circus. While walking along a street in Auckland, New Zealand he slipped on an orange peel, fell, broke his leg and fractured his jaw. Gangrene set in resulting in his leg having to be amputated. He died around two months later of complications from the infection.

Final Resting Place | Hillsborough Cemetery, Hillsborough, Auckland, New Zealand.

Lee, Brandon (Bruce)

Born | 01st February 1965

Died | 31st March 1993 (28)

Profession | Actor and Martial Artist.

Remembered for | Legacy of Rage (Movie). Kung Fu: The Movie (ABC TV show). Showdown in Little Tokyo (Movie). Rapid Fire (Movie). The Crow (Movie).

Cause of Death | Gunshot wound(s) (Accidental).

Details

Lee was accidentally shot in the abdomen by the tip of a dummy round lodged in the chamber of an improperly loaded prop gun fired by co-star Michael Massee while filming a scene for "The Crow" (Movie). The shooting was ruled an accident due to negligence.

Final Resting Place | Lake View Cemetery, Seattle, Washington (Next his father Bruce Lee).

Lee (Mister)

Born |

Died | 07th October 2010

Profession | Not known.

Remembered for | Not applicable.

Cause of Death | Injuries sustained in fall from height.

Details

A man known only as 'Mr Lee' who was a wheelchair user was recorded on CCTV ramming the doors of an elevator in a shopping mall in Daejeon, South Korea with his wheelchair.

The first two strikes loosened the doors while the third opened the doors and Lee went into the elevator shaft and fell around 5.8m/19ft to his death. He was apparently angry that he had just missed the elevator by a split-second as the doors were closed in front of him by a woman inside.

Final Resting Place | Unknown.

Lully, Jean-Baptiste

Born | 18th or 28th November 1632

Died | 22nd March 1687

Profession | Composer, Dancer and Instrumentalist.

Remembered for | Being considered a master of the French Baroque style. Working most of his life in the court of King Louis XIV (the Sun King).

Cause of Death | Gangrene.

Details

While vigorously conducting an orchestra during a performance of "Te Deum", Lully accidental pierced his foot with the staff he was using. Suffering from Gangrene in his leg he refused to have it amputated so he could still dance. The Gangrene spread through his body infecting his brain causing his death.

Final Resting Place | Notre-Dame-des-Victoires, Paris.

M

MacColl, Kirsty (Anna)

Born | 10th October 1959

Died | 18th December 2000 (41)

Profession | Singer and Songwriter.

Remembered for | There's a Guy Works Down the Chip Shop Swears He's Elvis (Song). A New England (Song). Days (Song). They Don't Know (Song). Fairytale of New York (Song).

Cause of Death | Injuries sustained when struck by a powerboat (Unlawfully killed).

Details

While on holiday in Cozumel, Mexico, MacColl and her sons went diving at the Chankanaab Reef, part of a National Marine Park in which watercraft were prohibited from entering. As they were surfacing after a dive MacColl saw a powerboat moving at high speed coming towards them. She pushed her son Jamie (15) out of the way but the boat ran over her causing severe chest injuries and she died instantly. Her son sustained minor head and rib injuries. The powerboat was owned by Guillermo Gonzalez Nova, the multimillionaire president of the Comecial Mexicana Supermarket chain who was on board with members of his family. Despite eyewitnesses stating that he was not at the controls, Boathand Jose Cen Yam said he was steering and was found guilty of culpable homicide.

He was sentenced to 34 months in prison, but under Mexican law he was allowed to pay 1,034 Pesos (around £61/$75US) in lieu of the prison sentence.

Final Resting Place | Cremated.

Mansfield, Martha (Erlich, Martha)

Born | 14th July 1899

Died | 30th November 1923 (24)

Profession | Actress.

Remembered for | Dr. Jekyll and Mr. Hyde (Movie). The Perfect Lover (Movie). Queen of the Moulin Rouge (Movie).

Cause of Death | Toxaemia and burns of all extremities.

Details

On 29th November, while on location in San Antonio, Texas on the film set of "The Warrens of Virginia", Mansfield had just finished shooting her scenes and was sitting in a car with fellow actors when someone struck a match and the lit head broke off landing on her clothing which burst into flames. Her Chauffeur was badly burned on his hands trying to remove her burning clothing. By the time the fire was put out she had sustained severe burns to her body. She was taken to the San Antonio Physicians and Surgeons Hospital but died from her injuries the following day.

Final Resting Place | Woodlawn Cemetery, The Bronx, New York.

Mantell, Thomas Francis

Born | 30th June 1922

Died | 07th January 1948 (25)

Profession | Pilot.

Remembered for | Not applicable.

Cause of Death | Injuries sustained in an aircraft crash.

Details

Mantell, a Captain in the USAF, was flying a single-engine North American P-51 Mustang near Goodman AFB in Kentucky while en route to Standiford in formation with three other aircraft. Around 13:30 police began to receive calls from individuals concerned about something in the sky above the town of Mannsville, Taylor County, Kentucky.

The unknown object was then sighted at about 14:40 by staff in the control tower at Godman AFB who contacted Mantell and the other pilots and requested that they investigate. Climbing to 15,000 feet Mantell and two other aircraft intercepted the object and he radioed, "The object is directly ahead and above me now, moving at about half my speed. It appears to be a metallic object or the reflection of the sun from a metallic object. It is of tremendous size. I'm still climbing. I'm trying to close in for a better look". Once they reached 22,000 feet the other two aircraft turned back as they were not equipped with oxygen. Mantell kept chasing the object and reached 30,000 feet where it is considered that he may have passed out due to lack of oxygen. His aircraft went into a steep dive and crashed into the front lawn of a farmhouse near Franklin, Kentucky.

A Richard T Miller later claimed that he was in the operations room at the time of the incident and stated that Mantell's last words were "My god I see people in this thing". The military eventually explained away the incident by recording the cause of the crash as the pilot losing consciousness due to lack of oxygen while chasing a weather balloon or the planet Venus.

Final Resting Place | Zachary Taylor National Cemetery, Louisville, Jefferson County, Kentucky, USA.

Mathilda of Austria (Archduchess)

Born | 25th January 1849

Died | 06th June 1867 (18)

Profession | Not known.

Remembered for | Not applicable.

Cause of Death | Second and third degree burns.

Details

On the 22nd May 1867 Mathilda set her gauze dress on fire while trying to hide a cigarette from her father who had forbidden her to smoke. She had been standing at the window in the Schloss Hetzendorf Palace when her father approached her and she placed the cigarette behind her dress, which immediately caught fire due to the very flammable material. Her back, arms, neck, and lower body were severely burned before the fire could be extinguished by her attendants. Despite being treated for her burns her injuries were to extensive and she died fifteen days later.

Final Resting Place | Imperial Crypt, Vienna, Austria.

McGuire, Ivan Lester

Born | c. 1953

Died | 05th April 1988 (35)

Profession | Parachutist, Skydiver, Instructor and Cameraman.

Remembered for | Making over 800 parachute jumps.

Cause of Death | Injuries sustained in a fall from height (Accidental).

Details

McGuire had been filming all day at the Franklin County Sport Parachute Center, Louisburg, North Carolina, with heavy video equipment strapped to his back. On his third jump to film an instructor and student he left the plane at 10,500 feet without his parachute. It was reported that on the previous jump he had to be reminded to put on his parachute. The pilot, Mark Luman, was responsible for ensuring each person had a parachute but it was thought that he mistook McGuire's bulky camera equipment for a parachute. Investigators consider that McGuire may have made the fatal error because he was tired or too preoccupied with the filming task.

Final Resting Place | Unknown.

McHugh, Grace

Born | c. 1898

Died | 01st July 1914 (16)

Profession | Actress.

Remembered for | Across the Border (Movie).

Cause of Death | Drowning (Accidental).

Details

McHugh was filming a scene for "Across the Border" when the boat she was in capsized and she fell into the fast flowing Arkansas River in Canon City, Colorado. Owen Carter, a cameraman, jumped in to rescue her and helped her to safety onto what he thought was a sandbar. However, once ashore both were sucked under by quicksand and drowned.

Final Resting Place | Golden Cemetery, Golden, Jefferson County, Colorado.

Meinsenheimer, Brenda Lee

Born | 20th March 1945

Died | 19th January 1967 (21)

Profession | Actress.

Remembered for | Dodge the White Hat (Movie short).

Cause of Death | Injuries sustained in a car crash.

Details

While filming a TV commercial for Pontiac in Thousand Oaks, California, Meinsenheimer along with cameraman Raffael John Esposito were killed when a camera boom suspended from an oncoming camera car crashed through the windscreen of their car.

Final Resting Place | Unknown.

Metcalfe, Earl

Born | 11th March 1889

Died | 26th January 1938 (38)

Profession | Actor.

Remembered for | The Airmail Pilot (Movie). The Fortune Hunter (Movie). While Justice Awaits (Movie). The Ship of Souls (Movie).

Cause of Death | Injuries sustained in a fall from height (Accidental).

Details

While on his fourth flying lesson at an airfield in Burbank, California, with his instructor, Roy Wilson, Metcalfe fell 2,000 feet from the aircraft after it suddenly went into a double roll.

Final Resting Place | Cremated.

Meyer, Monica

Born | 25th February 1910

Died | 20th March 1980 (70)

Profession | Not known.

Remembered for | Being the Mayor of Betterton, Maryland.

Cause of Death | Drowning (Accidental).

Details

While carrying out her own tests on the town of Betterton's sewage tank, Meyer lost her footing and fell into 15 feet of human waste. Officials stated that there would have been no chance of escape as the waste would have behaved just like quicksand.

Final Resting Place | Still Pond Cemetery, Still Pond, Kent County, Maryland.

Millan, Sergio

Born | c. 1961

Died | 14th January 2020 (59)

Profession | Grocer.

Remembered for | Not applicable.

Cause of Death | Crush injuries.

Details

Millan was alone in his apartment in Torreforta, Tarragona, Spain, when the force of an explosion at a petrochemical plant three kilometres away sent a one-ton iron plate (122cm/c. 4ft by 165cm/c. 5ft 4in) crashing through the window of the third floor apartment above him, resulting in his ceiling collapsing and crushing him to death. The plate was believed to be the top of a 20-ton reactor tank where ethylene oxide (used in detergents) was being produced.

Final Resting Place | Unknown.

Mitchell, Alex

Born | c. 1925

Died | 24th March 1975 (49/50)

Profession | Not known.

Remembered for | Not applicable.

Cause of Death | Heart attack.

Details

Mitchell had been laughing continuously for 25 minutes while watching The Goodies (TV show) episode "Kung Fu Kapers" at his home in Kings Lynn, Norfolk when he suffered a fatal heart attack. Mitchells' widow later sent a letter to the Goodies cast thanking them for making her husband's final moments so pleasant.

Final Resting Place | Unknown.

Mirro, Roger Joseph

Born | 04th August 1956

Died | 31st July 2013 (56)

Profession | Not known.

Remembered for | Not applicable.

Cause of Death | Injuries sustained when crushed by machinery.

Details

Mirro of South Clubhouse Drive, Palatine, Cook County, Illinois told a neighbour that he thought he had dropped his phone down the garbage chute and was going to look for it. He was later found crushed to death in a trash compactor.

Final Resting Place | Unknown.

Moliere
(Poquelin, Jean-Baptiste)

Born | 15th January 1622

Died | 17th February 1673 (51)

Profession | Actor, Playwright and Poet.

Remembered for | Tartuffe (Comedy play). The Misanthrope (Play). Don Juan (Novel). The School for Wives (Comedy play).

Cause of Death | Tuberculosis.

Details

During a production of his final play, Le Malade Imaginaire (The Imaginary Invalid), Moliere (who suffered from Pulmonary Tuberculosis) was seized by a violent coughing fit and suffered a haemorrhage.

He finished the play but then collapsed and died a few hours later. The superstition that green brings bad luck to actors is said to originate from the colour of his clothing at the time of his death.

Final Resting Place | Pere Lachaise Cemetery, Paris.

Moody, Jerome

Born | c. 1954

Died | 30th July 1985 (31)

Profession | Not known.

Remembered for | Not applicable.

Cause of Death | Drowning (Accidental).

Details

After celebrating the first drowning-free swimming season party, held at the New Orleans Recreation Department Center Swimming Pool, Lifeguards found the full clothed body of Moody at the bottom of the deep end of the pool. Around half of the 200 people at the party were said to have been Lifeguards, including four who were on duty that night.

Final Resting Place | Unknown.

Morrow, Victor (Morozoff, Victor)

Born | 14th February 1929

Died | 23rd July 1982 (53)

Profession | Actor and Director.

Remembered for | Combat (ABC TV show). Blackboard Jungle (Movie). Dirty Mary, Crazy Larry (Movie).

Cause of Death | Injuries sustained when struck by helicopter.

Details

Morrow was filming a scene for the "Twilight Zone" (Movie) in Indian Dunes, Santa Clarita, California, along with two child actors, 6 year old Renee Shin-Yi Chen and 7 year old Myca Dinh Le. A helicopter. a Bell UH-1B Huey (N87701) was hovering above them at 24 feet when heat from the special effect pyrotechnics damaged the tail rotor blades causing the helicopter to crash on top of them killing them all instantly. Morrow and Myca Dinh Le were decapitated and Renee Shin-Yi Chen was crushed by one of the helicopters struts.

Director John Landis, Pilot Dorsey Wingo, and three others were acquitted of involuntary manslaughter after a trial lasting almost nine months.

Final Resting Place | Hillside Memorial Park Cemetery, Culver City, California.

Murillo-Moncada, Larry Ely

Born | 22nd August 1984

Died | 28th November 2009 (25)

Profession | Supermarket employee.

Remembered for | Not applicable.

Cause of Death | Unable to establish.

Details

Murillo-Moncada, a supermarket worker in Council Bluffs, Iowa, is believed to have fallen into an 18in/45cm gap between a twelve feet high cooler and a wall and become trapped. His body was not discovered until January 2019 when the cooler was being moved three years after the closure of the No Frills Supermarket in 2016. Investigators believe that Murillo-Moncada climbed on top of the cooler, a place where employees sometimes went to hide when they wanted to take an unofficial break. He is thought to have fallen into the gap and became trapped. The noise from the coolers compressors could have concealed attempts by him to call for help. Numerous former employees had said that they could always smell something terrible in the area of the cooler.

Final Resting Place | Unknown.

𝒩

Nikaidoh, Hitoshi Christopher

Born | 27th April 1968

Died | 16th August 2003 (35)

Profession | Doctor.

Remembered for | Not applicable.

Cause of Death | Decapitation (Accidental).

Details

While Nikaidoh was boarding an elevator on the second floor of Christus St. Joseph's Hospital, Houston, Texas, the doors closed trapping his shoulders.

The elevator then began moving upwards and the ceiling sliced off most of his head, which fell inside the elevator. The elevator finally stopped four feet below the fifth floor trapping physicians assistant Karin Steinau inside for more than an hour. The cause of death was recorded as being due to multiple blunt force injuries to Nikaidoh's head and body. An investigation carried out by Chief Elevator Inspector Ron Steele uncovered 22 code violations, including burned resistors, closed connections left open, and a missing generator guard. The elevator was also a month past its annual inspection date despite having been worked on by maintenance crew's days earlier.

Final Resting Place | Restlands Memorial Park, Dallas, Texas.

O

O'Brien, Daniel John

Born | c. 1959

Died | 14th January 1990 (31)

Profession | Not known.

Remembered for | Not applicable.

Cause of Death | Injuries sustained from being sucked into a jet engine.

Details

O'Brien (an American tourist from Roselle, Illinois), while naked, climbed over two barbed wire fences, fought off four security guards, and stole their vehicle at Piarco International Airport, Trinidad (ICAO: TTPP). He then drove into a taxiing British Airways Boeing 747 smashing the vehicles top. He then struggled out of the wreckage, smeared grease on one of his shoulders that was bleeding, and jumped into one of the 747's engines.

Final Resting Place | Unknown.

O'Connor, Harry

Born | 28th August 1957

Died | 04th April 2002 (44)

Profession | Stuntman and Skydiver.

Remembered for | The stunts on The Perfect Storm (Movie). Aerial safety co-ordinator on Tomorrow Never Dies (Movie) and Charlie's Angels (Movie). Air Force One (Movie).

Cause of Death | Cervical fracture.

Details

O'Connor (stunt double for Vin Diesel) was in Prague in the Czech Republic filming the movie "xXx" when he hit a stone pillar of the Palacky Bridge, on the Vitava River, while being pulled at high speed on a paraglider. He died instantly when he broke his neck.

Final Resting Place | Unknown.

Otis Jr, James

Born | 05th February 1725

Died | 23rd May 1783 (58)

Profession | Lawyer and Legislator.

Remembered for | Being regarded as one of the most passionate and effective protectors of American rights during the 1760s.

Cause of Death | Struck by lightning.

Details

In 1769, at the height of his popularity, Otis was struck on the head by a Boston Custom-House official wielding a cane. For the rest of his life he suffered from bouts of mental instability and spent most of his time wandering the streets of Boston.

In 1783 while standing in the doorway of a friend's house during a thunderstorm in Andover, Essex County, Massachusetts, Otis died instantly when he was struck by lightning. He is reported to have told his sister, Mercy Otis Warren, sometime earlier "My dear sister, I Hope, when God Almighty in his righteous providence shall take me out of time into eternity that it will be by a flash of lightning".

Final Resting Place | Granary Burying Ground, Boston, Suffolk County, Massachusetts.

𝒫

Parsons, Gram
(Connor, Ingram Cecil)

Born | 05th November 1946

Died | 19th September 1973 (26)

Profession | Singer, Songwriter and Musician.

Remembered for | The Byrds (Group). Flying Burrito Brothers (Group). The International Submarine Band (Group).

Cause of Death | Drug overdose (Accidental).

Details

Parsons overdosed on morphine in room 8 at the Joshua Tree Inn (Twentynine Palms Highway, Joshua Tree, California) and was declared dead on arrival at the High Desert Memorial Hospital. The official cause of death was an accidental overdose of morphine and alcohol. Before his death Parsons had requested that he wanted to be cremated at Joshua Tree and his ashes scattered over Cap Rock (Joshua Tree National Park). However, Parsons step-father organised a private funeral in New Orleans without inviting any of his friends from the music industry. To fulfil Parsons wishes Phil Kaufman (Parsons' road manager) and Michael Martin (a friend of Kaufman's) stole his body from Los Angeles Airport by pretending to be undertakers using a borrowed hearse.

They then drove to Cap Rock and poured five gallons of oil into the coffin and threw a lit match inside which caused a massive fireball. They were arrested several days later but as there was no law against stealing a dead body they were only charged with stealing a coffin and fined $750 (£600).

Final Resting Place | Garden of Memories Cemetery, Metaire, Louisiana.

Phyall, David

Born | c. 1958

Died | 05th July 2008 (50)

Profession | Not known.

Remembered for | Not applicable.

Cause of Death | Decapitation (Suicide).

Details

After losing an eviction fight, Phyall (who had a history of suffering from mental illness and had attempted suicide in the past) plugged a chainsaw into the mains and put a timer on the socket. He then took a number of pills to render himself unconscious and rested the saw on his neck. When the chainsaw activated it decapitated him. The Coroner recorded a verdict of suicide.

Final Resting Place | Unknown.

Pinkerton, Allan

Born | 25th August 1819

Died | 01st July 1884 (64)

Profession | Detective and Spy.

Remembered for | Creating the Pinkerton National Detective Agency.

Cause of Death | Gangrene.

Details

While Pinkerton was walking his wife's poodle, the dog reportedly wrapped its leash around his legs causing him to trip and fall to the ground, where he severely bit his tongue. He died a few days later from a Gangrene infection of his tongue.

Final Resting Place | Graceland Cemetery, Chicago.

Q

Quinn, Philip

Born | c. 1980

Died | 28th November 2004 (24)

Profession | Not known.

Remembered for | Not applicable.

Cause of Death | Exsanguination. (Bleeding out).

Details

Quinn died when a lava lamp he was heating on a stove in the kitchen of his trailer home exploded, resulting in shards of glass embedding in his chest with one piercing his heart. There was no evidence of drug or alcohol use and his death was ruled an accident.

Final Resting Place | Unknown.

R

Randall, Jack
(Randall, Addison Byron Owen)

Born | 12th May 1906

Died | 16th July 1945 (39)

Profession | Actor and Singer.

Remembered for | Riders of the Dawn (Movie). Where the West Begins (Movie). Danger Valley (Movie). Covered Wagon Trails (Movie).

Cause of Death | Heart attack.

Details

Randall was championed as "the singing cowboy" but despite his singing ability, his movies were poorly received, said mainly to be due to poor production techniques. Randall's starring roles soon dried up and he moved into supporting roles. While filming a riding scene for "The Royal Mounted Rides Again" in Canoga Park, Los Angeles County he suffered a heart attack, fell from his horse and struck a tree. He died shortly afterwards.

Final Resting Place | Forest Lawn Memorial Park, Glendale, California.

Reichelt, Franz

Born | 16th October 1878

Died | 04th February 1912 (33)

Profession | Tailor and Inventor.

Remembered for | Being known as 'The Flying Tailor'.

Cause of Death | Injuries sustained in a fall from height.

Details

Despite being told by the authorities to use a mannequin Reichelt instead opted to jump from the Eiffel Tower, Paris, France wearing a parachute suit made from cloth that he had invented. The parachute failed to unfold and he fell 57m/187ft and hit the ground leaving a crater 15-20cm/6-7in deep.

Final Resting Place | Cremated.

Rhoads, Randy (Randall William)

Born | 06th December 1956

Died | 19th March 1982 (25)

Profession | Guitarist.

Remembered for | Being the guitarist in Quiet Riot (Group) and for Ozzy Osbourne (Singer).

Cause of Death | Injuries sustained in a plane crash.

Details

While stopped at Flying Baron Estates, Leesburg, Florida, to fix a faulty air conditioner, on Ozzy Osbourne's tour bus, the driver Andrew Aycock, a private pilot, took a single-engine Beech F35 Bonanza (N567LT) without permission.

As well as Rhoades, Rachel Youngblood the group's hairdresser joined Aycock. While in the air Aycock made attempts to "buzz" the tour bus. He made two successful close passes but on the third the wing clipped the top of the bus breaking it into two parts and sending the aircraft into an uncontrollable spin. The initial impact caused Rhoads' and Youngblood's heads to smash through the windscreen. It then hit a pine tree and crashed into a nearby garage and burst into flames. All three on board were killed instantly. The cause of the crash was determined to be poor judgement and clearance misjudgement by the pilot.

Final Resting Place | Mountain View Cemetery, San Bernardino, California.

S

Sagal, Boris

Born | 18th October 1923

Died | 22nd May 1981 (58)

Profession | Film and TV Director.

Remembered for | The Omega Man (Movie). The Name of the Game (Movie). Masada (Movie). Rich Man, Poor Man (TV show).

Cause of Death | Injuries sustained when struck by a helicopter.

Details

While alighting from a Bell 206B Jet Ranger helicopter (N58004) in the car park at Timberline Lodge, near Government Camp, Oregon, Sagal accidently walked into the tail rotor and was partially decapitated. He died five hours later in hospital. The NTSB report into the accident records "sunglare" as a condition present at the time.

Final Resting Place | Forest Lawn Memorial Park, Hollywood Hills, Hollywood.

Sky, Adam
(Neat, Adam Gary)

Born | 1976 or 1977

Died | 04th May 2019 (42)

Profession | DJ.

Remembered for | Being the third most popular DJ in Asia. The Guestlist (Radio show).

Cause of Death | Exsanguination (Bleeding out).

Details

While rushing to the aid of his assistant, Zoia Lukiantceva (who had fell 30 feet (10m) from a terrace and broken her leg), Sky crashed into a glass door and sustained a severe wound in his arm that cut into his artery. He was discovered the next day at the Hillstone Villas resort in South Kuta, Bali, Indonesia where he was staying having bled to death. Lukiantceva survived.

Final Resting Place | Unknown.

Staininger, Hans

Born | c. 1508

Died | 28th September 1567 (59)

Profession | Burgomaster (Mayor) of Braunau, Bavaria (now Austria).

Remembered for | His 4.5 feet (1.37m) long beard which he usually kept in a pouch.

Cause of Death | Cervical fracture.

Details

While Staininger was asleep in the Town Hall in Braunau a fire broke out. As he tried to escape he fell over his beard and broke his neck. His beard is displayed in the town's museum.

Final Resting Place | Unknown.

Stewart, Payne

Born | 30th January 1957

Died | 25th October 1999 (42)

Profession | Golfer.

Remembered for | Winning 11 PGA Tour events (including three major championships).

Cause of Death | Injuries sustained in a plane crash.

Details

While Stewart was flying from Orlando International to Dallas-Love Field on a twin-engine Gates Learjet 35 (N47BA) with three other passengers and two crew, all on board became incapacitated due to hypoxia.

Air Traffic Control (ATC) lost contact with the aircraft at 09:20 EDT and the aircraft was then intercepted by a number of USAF and ANG aircraft as it continued to fly northwest bound. The military pilots reported that the forward windshield of the Learjet was frosted or covered with condensation. They continued to observe as the aircraft left controlled flight and spiralled to the ground, impacting in an open field 12.5 miles (20km) west of Aberdeen, South Dakota killing all on board. The NTSB determined the probable cause as "incapacitation of the flight crew members as a result of their failure to receive supplemental oxygen following a loss of cabin pressurization, for undetermined reasons".

Final Resting Place | Doctor Phillips Cemetery, Orlando, Orange County, Florida.

Streeter, Bradley

Born | c. 2000

Died | 08th February 2020 (20)

Profession | Not known.

Remembered for | Not applicable.

Cause of Death | Injuries sustained in a fall from height (Accidental).

Details

Streeter was with friends when he placed himself on the railing of a viewing platform at the Cave Gardens sinkhole in Mount Gambier, South Australia, and then allegedly attempted a handstand. It is considered that he either lost his balance, or his grip, which resulted in him falling 98 feet down the sinkhole.

Final Resting Place | Two Wells Cemetery, Two Wells, South Australia.

Subramanian, Ravi

Born | c. 1961

Died | 16th December 2015 (54)

Profession | Chief Aircraft Engineer.

Remembered for | Not applicable.

Cause of Death | Injuries sustained from being sucked into a jet engine.

Details

Subramanian was sucked into the engine of an Air India Airbus A319 (VT-SCQ) twin-engine passenger airliner (on flight AI619 Mumbai to Hyderabad) as it was being pushed back from its stand and the engines were started. He had not realised that the aircraft had started to move. Subramanian died instantly.

Final Resting Place | Unknown.

T

Taylor, Henry

Born | c. 1812

Died | 24th October 1872 (60)

Profession | Pall Bearer.

Remembered for | Not applicable.

Cause of Death | Injuries sustained when crushed by a falling coffin.

Details

on the 19th October, while carrying a coffin in Kensal Green Cemetery in London, Taylor tripped over a side stone and stumbled.

The other pall bearers let go of the coffin and it fell on top of him, fracturing his jaw and ribs. He was taken to hospital but died of his injuries. A verdict of "accidental death" was recorded.

Final Resting Place | Unknown.

Thomas, Olive (Duffy, Olive R)

Born | 20th October 1894

Died | 10th September 1920 (25)

Profession | Actress.

Remembered for | A Girl Like That (Movie). Upstairs and Down (Movie). An Even Break (Movie). Heiress for a Day (Movie). The Flapper (Movie). Beatrice Fairfax (Movie).

Cause of Death | Poisoning (Accidental).

Details

on the 05th September 1920, Thomas mistakenly drank, from a flask, her husband's Syphilis medication (mercury bichloride). It was considered that as the label was in French she had mistaken the contents for drinking water. She was taken to the American Hospital, Neuilly-sur-Seine in Paris where she died five days later of acute Nephritis. Her death was ruled "accidental".

Final Resting Place | The Woodlawn Cemetery and Conservancy, Bronx, New York.

Thomas, Paul G

Born | c. 1940

Died | 11th August 1987 (47)

Profession | Businessman.

Remembered for | Not applicable.

Cause of Death | Asphyxiation (Accidental).

Details

Thomas, who was the co-owner of a Wool Mill in Thompson, Connecticut, died of suffocation after falling into one of the machines and becoming wrapped in 800 yards of wool.

Final Resting Place | Unknown.

U

Unknown

Born | Unknown.

Died | 22nd August 1878 (?)

Profession | Not known.

Remembered for | Being the first and only reliable case of a person being killed by a meteorite.

Cause of Death | Injuries sustained when struck by a meteorite.

Details

At around 20:30, as detailed in letters from high-ranking local government officials, above Cisane, a mountain village in the eastern part of the Kurdistan Region in Iraq near the city of Sulaymaniyah a large fireball lit up the skies, which then exploded causing large fragments to fall to the ground for ten minutes. The falling debris struck and killed one man and paralysed another.

Final Resting Place | Unknown.

Unknown

Born | c. 1965

Died | January 2019 (54)

Profession | Construction worker.

Remembered for | Not applicable.

Cause of Death | Heart failure.

Details

The unnamed 54-year-old male from Massachusetts, was eating a bag and a half of black liquorice every day for three weeks which resulted in low potassium levels (Hypokalemia) causing his heart to stop. Doctors, who said they were shocked and surprised at the cause of death, stated that a few weeks before his death the man had changed from red fruit-flavoured candy twists to another type made with black liquorice.

Final Resting Place | Unknown.

Unknown

Born | c. 1982

Died | May 2021 (39)

Profession | Not known.

Remembered for | Not applicable.

Cause of Death | Asphyxiation.

Details

The unnamed 39-year old male was found dead wedged upside down inside the hind leg of a paper-mache statue of a Stegosaurus outside the Cubic Building in the town of Santa Coloma de Gramenet, Catalonia, Spain. Local police considered that the individual may have crawled inside headfirst to retrieve his mobile phone but his leg got stuck trapping him.

They added that they did not suspect foul play and that he may have been trapped for a couple of days. His body was discovered after a local man and his son smelled a foul odour emitting from the statue.

Final Resting Place | Unknown.

𝒱

Vallandigham, Clement Laird

Born | 29th July 1820

Died | 17th June 1871 (50)

Profession | Lawyer and Politician.

Remembered for | Not applicable.

Cause of Death | Gunshot wound(s) (Accidental).

Details

While defending a man accused of murder in a court in Lebanon, Warren County, Ohio, Vallandigham began to demonstrate how he considered that the victim could have shot himself. In order to dramatise the scene he pulled out a gun (which he thought was unloaded) which accidentally discharged killing him. The accused was acquitted.

Final Resting Place | Woodland Cemetery and Arboretum, Dayton, Montgomery County, Ohio.

Van Gogh, Vincent

Born | 30th March 1853

Died | 29th July 1890 (37)

Profession | Post-impressionist Painter.

Remembered for | Creating, in just over a decade, nearly 2,100 artworks, including 860 oil paintings. Starry Night Over the Rhone (Painting). Still Life: Vase With Twelve Sunflowers (Painting). Van Gogh Self-Portrait (Painting). Irises (Painting). Self-portrait With a Bandage (Painting).

Cause of Death | Gunshot wound(s).

Details

On the 27th July, Van Gogh shot himself in the chest with a revolver. The bullet was deflected by a rib and then passed through his chest without doing any damage to his internal organs and was stopped by his spine. He managed to walk back to the Auberge Ravoux (located in the heart of the village of Auvers-sur-Oise) where he was staying and was treated by two doctors.

Although they could not remove the bullet he seemed in good spirits and they left him alone in his room smoking his pipe. However, within hours his health began to deteriorate due to an untreated infection caused by the wound and he died in the early hours of the 29th of July.

Final Resting Place | Auvers-sur-Oise Town Cemetery, Auvers-sur-Oise, France.

Vatel, Francois

Born | c. 1631

Died | 24th April 1671 (40)

Profession | Majordomo (Head Servant).

Remembered for | Being the Majordomo (the head servant) for Princes Louis II de Bourbon-Conde.

Cause of Death | Sword wound(s) (Suicide).

Details

Vatel was responsible for a banquet for 2,000 people hosted in honour of King Louis XIV at the Chateau de Chantilly (50km North of Paris). He became so distraught at the late delivery of the seafood (as well as other mishaps) that he killed himself with his sword. His body was found when a servant came to tell him the seafood had arrived.

Final Resting Place | Gourville Cemetery, Gourville, SW France.

W

Weldens, Barbara

Born | 17th April 1982

Died | 19th July 2017 (35)

Profession | Singer and Songwriter.

Remembered for | Le Grand H de l'homme (Album). Je ne Veux Pas de Ton Amour (Album).

Cause of Death | Electrocution (Accidental).

Details

Weldens was performing in a church in the town of Gourdon, SW France when she collapsed on stage and died of a cardiac arrest. An inquest determined that she had been electrocuted after apparently standing while barefooted on a defective piece of electrical equipment. It was known that she normal preferred performing barefooted.

Final Resting Place | Unknown.

Wertheim, Dick

Born | c. 1922

Died | 15th September 1983 (61)

Profession | Tennis linesman.

Remembered for | Not applicable.

Cause of Death | Subdural Hematoma (bleeding and increased pressure on the brain).

Details

On the 10th September 1983, Wertheim was sitting in a chair while officiating at a tennis match at the 1983 US Open in Flushing, New York, when an errant serve from Stefan Edberg (playing Patrick McEnroe) struck him in the groin. The force of the blow knocked him backwards and he fell out of his chair and struck his head on the hard-court surface. He was taken unconscious to Flushing Hospital and Medical Centre but died five days later.

Final Resting Place | Unknown.

Whinfrey, Stephen

Born | c. 1964

Died | 01st January 2015 (50)

Profession | Not known.

Remembered for | Not applicable.

Cause of Death | Asphyxiation (Accidental).

Details

Whinfrey's head became wedged down a rabbit hole while he was rabbiting in Squirrel Wood Scout Camp, near Doncaster in Yorkshire. His body, with only his legs and torso visible, was found on the 02nd January by a member of the public.

Final Resting Place | Unknown.

~180~

Williams, Robert

Born | 02nd May 1953

Died | 25th January 1979 (25)

Profession | Assembly worker.

Remembered for | Being the first human to be killed by a robot.

Cause of Death | Injuries sustained when struck by a robot.

Details

Williams, who worked on the production line at Ford Motor's Flat Rock plant in Michigan, was hit on the head by the arm of a one tonne robot. A court concluded that he died due to inadequate safety measures.

Final Resting Place | Unknown.

Williams, Tennessee (Thomas Lanier)

Born | 26th March 1911

Died | 25th February 1983 (71)

Profession | Playwright.

Remembered for | The Glass Menagerie (Stage play and Movie). A Street Car Named Desire (Stage play and Movie). Cat on a Hot Tin Roof (Stage play and Movie). The Night of the Iguana (Stage play and Movie).

Cause of Death | Asphyxiation (Accidental).

Details

Williams died in his suite at the Hotel Elysee in New York after accidently inhaling and swallowing a plastic cap from a bottle of eye drops or nasal spray.

Final Resting Place | Calvary Cemetery, St. Louis, Missouri.

Woolf, Ben (Benjamin Eric)

Born | 15th September 1980

Died | 23rd February 2015 (34)

Profession | Actor.

Remembered for | American Horror Story (TV show). Woggie (Movie). Dead Kansas (Movie).

Cause of Death | Stroke.

Details

On the 19th February, while crossing a road near Hollywood Boulevard, Woolf (who was 4ft 4in/1.3m) was struck by the sideview mirror of an SUV. He was taken to Cedars-Sinai Medical Center, Los Angeles where he died four days later of a stroke as a result of the head injuries he had sustained. Police later said that the driver was not arrested as Woolf was "jaywalking" when he was hit.

Final Resting Place | Cremated.

y

Yelchin, Anton

Born | 11th March 1989

Died | 19th June 2016 (27)

Profession | Actor.

Remembered for | Playing "Chekov" in Star Trek, Star Trek Into Darkness, and Star Trek Beyond (Movies). Green Room (Movie). Like Crazy (Movie). Hearts in Atlantis (Movie). Huff (TV show).

Cause of Death | Cardiac arrest after accidental blunt traumatic asphyxia.

Details

Yelchin was found crushed between a brick pillar and his Jeep Grand Cherokee in his driveway at his home in Studio City, California. It was considered that, when he got out of his car it rolled back down the driveway (which is on a steep incline) and trapped him against a pillar and a security fence.

Final Resting Place | Hollywood Forever Cemetery, Hollywood, Los Angeles.

Bibliography

Some of the resources used in compiling this publication

avherald.com

aviation-safety.net

Bell, Don | The Man Who Killed Houdini

biography.com

Britannica

British Library

British Newspaper Archive

Chronicling America

darwinawards.com

faa.gov

findagrave.com

Google News

gov.uk/aaib

Historical Newspapers Archives (US)
Historical Newspapers Archives (Worldwide)
hollywood.com
Hollywood Reporter

legacy.com
Library of Congress

National Library of Scotland
ntsb.org

planecrashinfo.com

thefamouspeople.com

wikipedia.com

~Also by the Authors~

♦ Untimely and Tragic Deaths of the Renowned, the Celebrated, and the Iconic: Featuring Ordinary Individuals Who Died in Bizarre Circumstances

♦ A Tome of Idioms (Complemented by some familiar proverbs and sayings) Their Meanings Explained

♦ 2001+ Humorous Quotes, Notes, and Anecdotes

♦ Revealed: The Hidden Meaning Behind the Lyrics of 501 Classic and Popular Songs

♦ Short Finals (Aviation Adventure)

♦ The Last Question (Science Fiction)

♦ The Little Book of Big Excuses (420 Hilarious Excuses)

♦ The Little Book of Superstitions Omens & Signs (Their meanings and origins explained)

All publications are available in the Amazon Bookstore as an ebook or paperback.

We endeavour to achieve accuracy by only including the facts as known at the time of writing. If you see something that is not quite right, or you have any comments or questions then please email us at us at villageearthbooks@gmail.com. Thank You. Brian and Valerie.

Beginning today, treat everyone you meet as if they were going to be dead by midnight. Extend to them all the care, kindness, and understanding you can muster, and do it with no thought of any reward. Your life will never be the same again,

-Augustine 'Og' Mandino (Author)-

Printed in Great Britain
by Amazon